FARMSTAND FAVORITES

Berries

Over 75 Farm Fresh Recipes

Farmstand Favorites: Berries
Text copyright © 2011 Hatherleigh Press

Hatherleigh Press is committed to preserving and protecting the natural resources of the Earth. Environmentally responsible and sustainable practices are embraced within the company's mission statement.

Hatherleigh Press is a member of the Publishers Earth Alliance, committed to preserving and protecting the natural resources of the planet while developing a sustainable business model for the book publishing industry.

This book was edited and designed in the village of Hobart, New York. Hobart is a community that has embraced books and publishing as a component of its livelihood. There are several unique bookstores in the village. For more information, please visit www.hobartbookvillage.com.

www.hatherleighpress.com

DISCLAIMER
This book offers general cooking and eating suggestions for educational purposes only. In no case should it be a substitute nor replace a healthcare professional. Consult your healthcare professional to determine which foods are safe for you and to establish the right diet for your personal nutritional needs.

Library of Congress Cataloging-in-Publication Data is available upon request.
ISBN: 978-1-57826-375-2

All Hatherleigh Press titles are available for bulk purchase, special promotions, and premiums. For information about reselling and special purchase opportunities, please call 1-800-528-2550 and ask for the Special Sales Manager.

Cover Design by Nick Macagnone
Photography by Catarina Astrom
Interior Design by Nick Macagnone

10 9 8 7 6 5 4 3 2 1

Improve your life. Change your world.

Acknowledgments

Hatherleigh Press would like to extend a special thank you to Jo Brielyn—without your hard work and creativity this book would not have been possible.

Table of Contents

All About Berries

When describing the many benefits of berries, the saying "Good things come in small packages" comes to mind. Although modest in size, berries contain a substantial amount of nutritional power. Not only do they pack a tasty punch, they are also good for you. The same pigments that give berries their vibrant hues of blues, purples, and reds also make them excellent for your health.

Here are some of the most common types of berries:

- Strawberries
- Blueberries
- Blackberries
- Cranberries
- Gooseberries
- Currants
- Raspberries
- Huckleberries

Berries contain high levels of *phytonutrients*—chemicals that are found in plants and believed to promote health. Since phytonutrients are most concentrated in the skin or peel of vegetables and fruits, berries are a great source due to their edible skins.

Berries such as blackberries, blueberries, raspberries, cranberries, and strawberries also contain *flavonoids*, which aid in the prevention of heart disease, stroke, and some forms of cancer. Berries are also high in nutrients and vitamins such as antioxidants, fiber, vitamin C, and manganese.

Much like other fruits and vegetables, berries start to lose nutrients once they have been picked. To reduce the time between when they are harvested and consumed, try to grow your own berries, pick them from a nearby berry farm, or buy them from a local farmstand. This will help you reap the greatest health benefits and the optimal flavors from your berries.

Keep these tips in mind when picking your own berries:

- **Pick berries early in the morning while it's still cool and the sun hasn't had time to soften them.** The next best time to pick is early in the evening when the sun is setting.

- **Look for berries hidden under leaves.** They are usually in the best condition.

- **Use both hands to pluck the berries to prevent crushing or bruising them.** Hold the branch or vine with one hand, and pick the berries with the other. Keep the stems and hulls on the fruit.

- **Pick only fully ripened berries that are firm and deeply colored.** They should not have green or white on the tips.

- **Avoid piling berries too high in the basket, or the ones on the bottom will get crushed.** Berries must be handled gently.

Here are some tips for storing berries:

- **Do not store berries in their original container.** Instead, remove and sort out any moldy or overripe ones. Then place the remaining berries in a loosely covered container.

- **Do not wash berries until right before using them.**

- **Do not allow berries to sit in the sun or heat.** Store them in a refrigerator set at 32° - 40°F.

- **For long-term storage, berries can be frozen in an airtight container.** Those prepared without sugar should be used within 3 months. Berries prepared with sugar or any other sweetener can be kept for close to a year.

- **Berries can also be pickled or preserved into a variety of jellies, jams, salsas, and chutneys.**

Did you know?

- North America is the leading blueberry producer and accounts for almost 90% of the world's production.

- Blueberries change colors during cooking. Acidic foods like vinegar make blueberries turn red. When mixed with an alkaline substance such as baking soda, the blueberries often turn greenish-blue.

- The small, yellow seed-like pieces (called achenes) on the surface of a strawberry are the real fruit of the plant. The red pulp of the berry is actually the shell.

- The pigmentation of the black raspberry is so powerful that the USDA used the berry's juice to stamp meat products for over 40 years.

- Cranberries bounce and float! The fruit has small air pockets inside that make them bounce when they are ripe. It also causes them to float on water.

- Not all raspberries are red. They also come in various shades of purple, black, and gold.

- Blueberries have no cholesterol or fat and are low in calories—only 84 calories for a whole cup.

Breakfast

Strawberry Omelet

Ingredients:

3 eggs

Pinch salt

2 tablespoons cold water

1 pint strawberries

3 tablespoons sugar

Directions:

Separate the whites and yolks of 2 eggs. Beat the whites to a stiff froth. Mix the yolks with a pinch of salt and the cold water. Pour the yolk mixture slowly into the beaten whites while beating constantly. Grease the bottom of a pan with non-stick spray or a small amount of butter. Pour in the eggs, cover, and cook for 3 minutes Loosen the omelet; if it sticks in some places to the pan, slip a broad-bladed knife underneath the omelet, lift it up on the side it sticks, and slip a small piece of butter underneath it; as soon as the omelet is loose, cover it again, and cook it until you can touch the top with your finger without any of the omelet adhering to it, then fold it over and slip it onto a plate. Wash and drain the strawberries, mash them with a fork, and add 3 tablespoons of sugar. When the omelet is baked, put part of the strawberries over the omelet, and fold. Pour the remaining strawberries around it and serve.

Oatmeal Pecan Waffles
(or Pancakes)
(Courtesy of NHLBI, part of NIH and HHS)

Ingredients:

Waffles:

1 cup whole-wheat flour

½ cup quick-cooking oats

2 teaspoons baking powder

1 teaspoon sugar

¼ cup unsalted pecans, chopped

2 large eggs, separated (for pancakes, see note)

1½ cups fat-free (skim) milk

1 tablespoon vegetable oil

Fruit Topping:

2 cups fresh strawberries, rinsed, stems removed, and cut in half

1 cup fresh blackberries, rinsed

1 cup fresh blueberries, rinsed

1 teaspoon powdered sugar

Directions:

Preheat waffle iron. Combine flour, oats, baking powder, sugar, and pecans in a large bowl. Combine egg yolks, milk, and vegetable oil in a separate bowl, and mix well. Add liquid mixture to the dry ingredients, and stir together. Do not over mix; mixture should be a bit lumpy. Whip egg whites to medium peaks. Gently fold egg whites into batter (for pancakes, see note below). Pour batter into preheated waffle iron, and cook until the waffle iron light signals it's done or steam stops coming out of the iron. (A waffle is perfect when it is crisp and well-browned on the outside with a moist, light, airy and fluffy inside.) (Or make pancakes.) Add fresh fruit topping and a light dusting of powdered sugar to each waffle, and serve.

Note: For pancakes, do not separate eggs. Mix whole eggs with milk and oil, then combine with the dry ingredients.

Strawberry Crêpes with Honey Suzette Sauce

(Courtesy of the National Honey Board)

Ingredients:

Honey Suzette Sauce:

½ cup honey
½ cup orange juice
1 tablespoon lemon juice
2 teaspoons grated orange peel
1½ teaspoons grated lemon peel
1½ teaspoons cornstarch
1 tablespoon butter or margarine
6 Low-Fat Honey Crêpes

Low-Fat Honey Crêpes:

2 cups fat-free milk
1 cup all-purpose flour
2 egg whites
1 egg
1 tablespoon honey
1 tablespoon vegetable oil
⅛ teaspoon salt
1 pint lemon sorbet or low-fat lemon yogurt
1½ cups fresh strawberries, sliced

Directions:

Honey Suzette Sauce:

In a small saucepan, whisk together honey, orange juice, lemon juice, orange peel, lemon peel, and cornstarch until well blended and cornstarch is dissolved. Bring mixture to a boil over medium-high heat, whisking occasionally; cook until mixture thickens. Remove from heat. Whisk in butter or margarine. Cool to room temperature or refrigerate until ready to use.

Low-Fat Honey Crêpes:

Combine all ingredients in blender or food processor; blend until smooth. Rub 8-inch non-stick skillet with oiled paper towel or spray lightly with non-stick cooking spray; heat over medium-high heat. Spoon 3 to 4 tablespoons crêpe batter into skillet, tilting and rotating skillet to cover evenly with batter. Cook until edges begin to brown. Turn crêpe over and cook until lightly browned. Remove crêpe to plate to cool. Repeat process with remaining batter. Crêpes may be refrigerated for 3 days or frozen up to 1 month in an airtight container.

To assemble the Strawberry Crepes with Honey Suzette Sauce:

Press 1 crêpe into each of 6 ramekins or bowls to form a cup. Fill each with 1 scoop of sorbet. Top each with ¼ cup sliced strawberries and 2 to 3 tablespoons Honey Suzette Sauce.

Makes 6 servings.

Honey Morning Muffins

(Courtesy of the National Honey Board)

Ingredients:

Muffins:

2½ cups 100% bran cereal

1¼ cups buttermilk

½ cup Clover honey

⅓ cup vegetable oil

½ tablespoon grated orange peel

2 eggs

⅔ cup dried cranberries

1½ cups flour

¼ cup brown sugar

4 teaspoons baking powder

¼ teaspoon salt

½ cup chopped pecans, optional

Honey Orange Butter

Honey Orange Butter:

½ cup butter, softened

¼ cup honey

1 tablespoon grated orange peel

Directions:

Muffins:

Preheat oven to 375°F and line 12 muffin tins with paper wrappers. Stir the cereal and buttermilk together in a large bowl; let stand for 5 minutes to soften cereal. Add honey, oil, orange peel, and eggs to bowl. Stir until combined, then add cranberries. Mix all dry ingredients in a small bowl and add to cereal, mixing just until combined. Stir in pecans, if desired, and spoon into prepared muffin tins. Muffin tins will be very full. Bake for 20 to 25 minutes or until golden brown and cooked through. Serve with Honey Orange Butter.

Makes 12 muffins.

Honey Orange Butter:

Stir together butter, honey, and grated orange peel. Store in refrigerator, tightly covered.

Breakfast Berry Corn Cakes

Ingredients:
½ cup corn meal
1 cup flour
1 cup milk
½ cup sugar
1½ teaspoons baking powder
1 egg
1 tablespoon melted butter
½ cup fresh berries (raspberries, strawberries, blueberries, or cranberries will work best)

Directions:
Mix together all ingredients except for the flour. Pour into mini muffin tins. Using a fork, lightly sprinkle flour over the corn cakes. Bake at 400°F for approximately 20 minutes or until brown.

Strawberry Banana Yogurt Parfait

(Courtesy of NHLBI, part of NIH and HHS)

Ingredients:

4 cups light (no-sugar-added) fat-free vanilla yogurt
2 large bananas (about 2 cups), sliced
2 cups fresh strawberries, sliced (or thawed frozen fruit)
2 cups graham crackers, crumbled
½ cup fat-free whipped topping, optional

Directions:

To make the parfait, spoon 1 tablespoon of yogurt into the bottom of each 8-ounce wine or parfait glass. Top the yogurt with 1 tablespoon sliced bananas, 1 tablespoon sliced strawberries, and ¼ cup graham crackers.

Repeat the yogurt, banana, strawberry, and graham cracker layers.

Top with a rounded tablespoon of fat-free whipped topping, if desired. Serve the parfait immediately, or cover each glass with plastic wrap and chill for up to 2 hours before serving.

Rhubarb-Strawberry Parfait

(Courtesy of the American Institute for Cancer Research,
www.aicr.org)

Ingredients:

1 pint strawberries, hulled and thickly sliced
½ pound fresh rhubarb, cut into 1½-inch pieces
¼ cup water
¼ cup orange juice
¼ cup sugar
1 vanilla bean, split lengthwise
1½ cups fat-free plain yogurt
1 teaspoon pure vanilla extract
1 teaspoon sugar, preferably superfine, optional

Directions:

Combine strawberries, rhubarb, water, orange juice, sugar, and vanilla bean in a heavy, medium saucepan. Bring to a boil over medium heat, stirring to dissolve the sugar. Reduce heat, cover, and simmer until fruit is very soft, about 10 minutes. Put mixture in a bowl and refrigerate until cold, about 4 hours.

Mix yogurt and vanilla until well combined. Taste and stir in superfine sugar (if desired). Chill until serving time.

To serve, layer yogurt mixture and strawberry-rhubarb mixture alternately into wineglasses or parfait glasses, ending with fruit. Parfaits can be prepared a few hours ahead and refrigerated.

Gooseberry Soufflé

Ingredients:
3 pints gooseberries
½ pint milk
4 eggs
3 ounces water
Sugar to taste

Directions:

Stew the gooseberries with water until quite soft. Add sugar
to taste. Rub the fruit through a coarse sieve and place into a
pie-dish. Warm the milk over medium heat. Beat the egg yolks
and mix them with the warmed milk. Pour the mixture over the
gooseberries and mix well. Bake in a moderate oven until set. In
the meantime, beat the whites of the eggs to a stiff froth, adding
sugar to taste. Lay this over the soufflé a few minutes before it
is done, and let it set in the oven. Serve immediately.

Strawberry-Blueberry Muffins

(Courtesy of the American Institute for Cancer Research,
www.aicr.org)

Ingredients:

3 tablespoons canola oil
⅓ cup unsweetened applesauce
½ cup sugar
2 eggs
1 teaspoon vanilla
1 cup fresh blueberries
1 cup chopped fresh strawberries
1 cup whole-wheat flour
1 cup unbleached all-purpose flour
2 teaspoons baking powder
¼ teaspoon salt
½ cup fat-free milk
Canola oil spray

Directions:

Preheat oven to 375°F. Spray 12-cup muffin tin with canola oil
and set aside. In medium bowl, whisk together oil, applesauce,
sugar, and eggs. Add vanilla, blueberries, and strawberries.
In separate bowl, blend together flours, baking powder, and
salt. Fold in half flour mixture, then half milk. Add remaining
flour and milk, folding in just until blended. Scoop batter into
prepared tins. Bake 25-30 minutes or until golden brown and
inserted toothpick comes out dry. Allow muffins to cool for 20
minutes before removing from pan.

Oatmeal Pancakes with Cranberries

(Courtesy of the American Institute for Cancer Research,
www.aicr.org)

Ingredients:

½ cup all-purpose flour
¼ cup whole-wheat flour
¼ teaspoon salt
1 tablespoon sugar
½ teaspoon baking powder
¾ teaspoon baking soda
¾ cup quick-cooking (not
instant) oats

2 egg whites, lightly beaten
1 cup plain low-fat yogurt
1 cup low-fat milk
1 teaspoon vanilla
2 tablespoons canola oil
½ cup dried cranberries
Powdered sugar, optional
Juice of 1 lemon, optional
Cooking spray

Directions:

Preheat the oven to 200°F. In a medium bowl, sift together all-purpose and whole-wheat flours. Add the remaining dry ingredients and mix well. In a separate bowl, beat the egg whites, yogurt, milk, vanilla, and oil. Add the wet ingredients to the dry ingredients, making sure not to over-mix. Stir in the cranberries. For the very best results, allow the batter to rest, covered, in the refrigerator for 30 minutes. Spray a griddle or large, flat pan with cooking spray. Heat to medium-high. Pour ¼ cup batter for each pancake and cook for approximately 2 to 3 minutes. When bubbles appear on the upper surface, flip the pancakes. Continue cooking until the second side is golden brown, about 2 minutes. As you make more pancakes, keep the finished pancakes in the warmed oven on a cookie sheet, separated with parchment paper. When ready to serve, lightly dust pancakes with powdered sugar and a squeeze of fresh lemon juice.

Bulgur with Apples, Currants and Toasted Pecans

(Courtesy of the American Institute for Cancer Research,
www.aicr.org)

Ingredients:
1 medium unpeeled apple, minced
⅓ cup currants
⅛ teaspoon cinnamon
1 cup dried bulgur, cooked according to package directions
1 cup plain or vanilla-flavored soy milk, heated
½ cup maple syrup
2 tablespoons finely chopped pecans

Directions:
In a small bowl, combine apple, currants, and cinnamon; set aside. In medium saucepan, prepare bulgur. Spoon bulgur evenly into 4 bowls. Pour warm soy milk evenly over bulgur; drizzle with maple syrup. Spoon apple mixture evenly on top; sprinkle with pecans. Serve immediately.

Serve this warm treat for breakfast instead of the traditional oatmeal.

Soups & Salads

Scandinavian Fruit Soup

Ingredients:
1 cup dried apricots
1 cup dried sliced apples
1 cup dried pitted prunes
1 cup dried cranberries
1 cup canned pitted red cherries
½ cup quick cooking tapioca
1 cup grape juice
3 cups water
½ cup orange juice
¼ cup lemon juice
1 tablespoon orange peel, grated
½ cup brown sugar

Directions:
Combine all dried fruits, cherries, tapioca, grape juice, and water in a slow cooker. Cover and cook on low for 8 hours. Before serving, stir in orange and lemon juices, orange peel, and brown sugar. Serve warm as soup or dessert. Serve chilled with frozen vanilla yogurt.

Jewish Fruit Soup

Ingredients:
½ pound plums
½ pound cherries
½ pound red currants
½ pound raspberries
1 pint water
1 egg yolk
Sugar to taste

Directions:
Wash all fruit and boil them to a pulp in the pint of water. Let it cool slightly and then stir in the beaten yolk of an egg and sugar to taste. Strain the soup. Serve cold.

Russian Fruit Salad

Ingredients:

2 cups peaches, peeled, pitted and sliced
2 cups pineapple, sliced
2 cups apricots, peeled, pitted and sliced
2 cups strawberries, sliced
2 cups raspberries
Juice of 2 lemons and 2 oranges
1 cup water
1 pound sugar
½ teaspoon powdered cinnamon
Grated rind from 1 lemon
1 cup red wine
½ glass rum

Directions:

Wash and prepare all the fruit and combine in a bowl. Prepare
a syrup from the lemon and orange, water, sugar, cinnamon,
lemon rind, red wine, and rum. Boil this syrup for five minutes
and pour over the fruit. Toss the fruit from time to time until
cool. Place on ice and serve cold.

Rainbow Fruit Salad
(Courtesy of NHLBI, part of NIH and HHS)

Ingredients:
1 large mango, peeled and diced
2 cups fresh blueberries
2 nectarines, unpeeled and sliced
2 cups halved fresh strawberries
2 cups seedless grapes
2 bananas, sliced
1 kiwifruit, peeled and diced
⅓ cup fresh orange juice
2 tablespoons lemon juice
1½ tablespoons honey
¼ teaspoon ground ginger
Dash nutmeg

Directions:
Prepare the fruit and place in a large bowl. Combine orange juice, lemon juice, honey, ginger, and nutmeg in a small bowl. Whisk together until well combined. Just before serving, pour honey orange sauce over the fruit.

Autumn Salad
(Courtesy of NHLBI, part of NIH and HHS)

Ingredients:
1 Granny Smith apple, rinsed and sliced thinly (with skin)
2 tablespoons lemon juice
5 cups mixed lettuce greens (or your favorite lettuce), rinsed
½ cup dried cranberries
¼ cup walnuts, chopped
¼ cup unsalted sunflower seeds
⅓ cup low-fat raspberry vinaigrette dressing

Directions:
Sprinkle lemon juice on the apple slices. Mix the lettuce, cranberries, apple, walnuts, and sunflower seeds in a bowl. Toss with raspberry vinaigrette dressing, to lightly cover the salad, and serve.

Marinated Edamame Salad

Ingredients:

Salad Dressing:

2 tablespoons parsley, minced
2 tablespoons olive oil
1 tablespoon honey
2 tablespoons water
¼ cup Dijon mustard
¼ cup lemon juice
2 cloves garlic, minced
¼ cup white wine vinegar
¼ teaspoon each basil, marjoram, rosemary, thyme, black pepper, and grated lemon peel

Salad:

2 cups lightly cooked green beans, cut into bite-sized pieces with ends trimmed
2 cups cooked and shelled edamame
¼ cup diced green onion
½ cup chopped red bell pepper
½ cup diced celery
½ cup chopped cucumber
2 cups romaine lettuce, washed
1 cup chopped carrots
⅓ cup dried cranberries

Directions:

Salad Dressing:

Whisk together the dressing ingredients; adjust seasonings to taste. Set aside.

Salad:

In a salad bowl, toss together all of the salad ingredients, except the lettuce. Whisk dressing again, pour over salad mixture, and toss. Cover and refrigerate at least one hour. When ready to serve, arrange lettuce on salad plates and top with marinated bean mixture.

Note: Fresh herbs may be substituted for the dried herbs listed above. When substituting fresh herbs, use approximately ½ teaspoon of each herb.

Summer Greens Salad with Sweetened Dried Cranberries and Cranberry Vinaigrette

(Courtesy of Cape Cod Cranberry Growers' Association, Carver, MA, www.cranberries.org)

Ingredients:

Vinaigrette:
¼ cup extra-virgin olive oil
2 tablespoons cranberry juice cocktail
1 tablespoon apple cider vinegar
1 tablespoon balsamic vinegar
2 teaspoons minced shallots
Salt and pepper to taste

Salad:
¼ cup walnut pieces, lightly toasted
2 cups mesclun greens, washed
1 head Belgian endive, yellow tipped, cored, and cut lengthwise into narrow strips
½ cup red onion, sliced in lengths
1 bunch watercress, washed
¼ cup sweetened dried cranberries

Directions:

Vinaigrette:

In small bowl whisk together the olive oil, cranberry juice cocktail, vinegars, and shallots. Season with salt and pepper to taste. Let stand for at least ½ hour to allow flavors to blend.

Salad:

In small dry frying pan, over medium heat, toast the walnuts, shaking the pan often, until brown and aromatic. Transfer to small bowl and set aside. Divide the mesclun greens among four individual salad plates. Top with cut endive, onion, and watercress. Add toasted walnut pieces and sweetened dried cranberries. Top with 2 tablespoons of vinaigrette.

Makes 4 servings.

Tropical Fruit Salad with Guava Sauce

Ingredients:
2 bananas, sliced
1 ripe pear, sliced
4 kiwis, peeled and sliced
2 cups sliced strawberries
2 feijoas, sliced (optional)
2 tablespoons orange juice concentrate
1 ripe guava

Directions:
Combine all of the ingredients, except for the juice and guava, in a large serving bowl. Peel and slice the guava into quarters and place in a blender with the orange juice concentrate. Puree until smooth. Pour the mixture through a sieve to remove the seeds and pour over the fruit salad.

Ginger-Carrot Salad with Cranberries

(Courtesy of the American Institute for Cancer Research, www.aicr.org)

Ingredients:

1 tablespoon freshly squeezed lemon juice
½ teaspoon honey
1 teaspoon freshly grated or finely minced ginger
⅛ teaspoon cinnamon
2 cups grated or julienned carrots (can use part cabbage)
¼ cup dried cranberries
2 tablespoons sliced almonds or peanuts
Pinch salt

Directions:

In medium bowl, whisk together lemon juice, honey, ginger, cinnamon, and salt. Toss with carrots (and cabbage, if using) and cranberries. Garnish with sliced almonds or peanuts and serve.

Avocado and Fruit Salad Dressing

Ingredients:
2 red delicious apples, cut into ½-inch cubes
1 teaspoon lemon juice
2 avocados, cut into ½-inch cubes
2 kiwi fruits, sliced
1 banana sliced
1 pint strawberries, sliced
1 pint blueberries
1 tablespoon honey
¼ teaspoon mace (East Indian spice similar to nutmeg)

Directions:
Place apples in a bowl with lemon juice to keep from browning.
Add all other ingredients. Gently mix fruit salad topping. Serve
on top of waffles, with or without liquid syrup.

Entrées

Baked Pork Chops with Apple Cranberry Sauce

(Courtesy of NHLBI, part of NIH and HHS)

Ingredients:

Pork Chops:

4 boneless pork chops
(about 3 ounces each)
¼ teaspoon ground black pepper
1 medium orange, rinsed, for
¼ teaspoon zest (use a grater
to take a thin layer of skin off
the orange; save the orange for
garnish)
½ tablespoon olive oil

Sauce:

¼ cup low-sodium chicken broth
1 medium apple, peeled and
grated (about 1 cup)
(use a grater to make thin
layers of apple)
½ cinnamon stick (or ⅛
teaspoon ground cinnamon)
1 bay leaf
½ cup dried cranberries
½ cup 100% orange juice

A wonderful fruit sauce adds the perfect touch to these pork chops— try serving with a side of brown rice and steamed broccoli.

Directions:

Pork Chops:

Preheat oven to 350°F. Season pork chops with pepper and orange zest. In a large sauté pan, heat olive oil over medium heat. Add pork chops, and cook until browned on one side, about 2 minutes. Turn over and brown the second side, an additional 2 minutes. Remove pork chops from the pan, place them on a non-stick baking sheet, and put in the oven to cook for an additional 10 minutes (to a minimum internal temperature of 160°F).

Sauce:

Add chicken broth to the sauté pan and stir to loosen the flavorful brown bits. Set aside for later. Meanwhile, place grated apples, cinnamon stick, and bay leaf in a small saucepan. Cook over medium heat until the apples begin to soften. Add cranberries, orange juice, and saved broth with flavorful brown bits. Bring to a boil, and then lower to a gentle simmer. Simmer for up to 10 minutes, or until the cranberries are plump and the apples are tender. Remove the cinnamon stick. Peel the orange used for the zest, and cut it into eight sections for garnish. Serve one pork chop with ¼ cup of sauce and two orange segments.

Sweet & Kicky Meatballs

(Courtesy of Cape Cod Cranberry Growers' Association, Carver, MA, www.cranberries.org)

Ingredients:

Meatballs:

1 pound lean ground beef
½ teaspoon salt
⅔ cup fresh bread crumbs
¼ teaspoon ground pepper
1 egg, slightly beaten
1 tablespoon Worcestershire sauce
1 tablespoon minced dried onion
1 tablespoon minced fresh parsley
2 cups or 1 (13¾ oz.) can beef broth

Cranberry Sauce:

1 (8 oz.) can whole berry cranberry sauce
¼ cup brown sugar
2 tablespoons canned chopped green chilies
¼ cup apple jelly

Directions:

Meatballs:

Combine all ingredients except broth in large bowl. Divide by quarter cups and shape into balls. Heat broth in large skillet. Cook meatballs, turning once, about 10 minutes. Drain well on paper towels. Place in oven proof covered casserole and top with Cranberry Sauce.

Bake in 350°F oven for 30 minutes.

Cranberry Sauce:

In small saucepan combine all ingredients, heating until jelly melts and ingredients are well combined. Pour over meatballs before baking.

Optional Garnish: Put dollop of sour cream on top and sprinkle with buttered breadcrumbs (cook ½ cup fresh breadcrumbs with 1 tablespoon butter in skillet until golden). Serve with baked potato, vegetable, and tossed salad.

Roasted Honey-Pepper Pork
(Courtesy of the National Honey Board)

Ingredients:
Pork:
2½ pounds boneless pork loin roast
¼ cup honey
2 tablespoons Dijon mustard
2 tablespoons crushed mixed peppercorns*
½ teaspoon thyme, crushed
½ teaspoon salt
Honey Cranberry Relish
Fresh thyme and cranberries, for garnish

Honey Cranberry Relish:
1 medium orange
12 ounces fresh whole cranberries
¾ cup honey

Directions:
Pork:
Carefully score roast ½-inch deep completely around, taking care not to cut the string holding roast together. Combine all remaining ingredients; mix well. Spoon or brush ⅔ of honey mixture over pork to coat. Place meat on roasting rack in baking pan. Roast at 300°F for 1 hour; brush with remaining honey mixture and cook about 45 minutes or until thermometer inserted into thickest part registers 170°F. Cool 10 minutes before slicing. Garnish with fresh thyme and cranberries. Serve with Honey Cranberry Relish.

Makes 8 servings.

Tip: Line baking pan with aluminum foil for easy clean-up.

Honey Cranberry Relish:
Quarter and slice unpeeled orange, removing seeds. Coarsely chop orange and cranberries. Place in medium saucepan and stir in honey. Bring to a boil over medium-high heat and cook 3 to 4 minutes. Cool. Makes ¼ cup.

*Black or white peppercorns can be substituted.

Ginger-Cran Leek Glazed Salmon

(Courtesy of Cape Cod Cranberry Growers' Association, Carver, MA, www.cranberries.org)

Ingredients:

2 cups whole cranberries
½ cup brown sugar
1 tablespoon fresh ginger (or ½ teaspoon dried)
1 leek, clean well and cut in rings
1 tablespoon olive oil
1 pound salmon

Directions:

Gently cook cranberries, sugar, and ginger until cranberries are soft (5–10 minutes). Sauté leek in oil. Combine leek and cranberries, then ladle over salmon. Broil salmon to your liking (best if cooked medium rare). Can be served with rice.

Chicken Breast Stuffed with Wild Rice and Cranberry Stuffing

(Courtesy of Cape Cod Cranberry Growers' Association, Carver, MA, www.cranberries.org)

Ingredients:

Chicken:

6 chicken breast halves, cleaned and tenders removed

Wild Rice and Cranberry Stuffing

Egg wash (3 eggs in bowl, beaten with fork)

Flour with salt and pepper added to taste

2 tablespoons olive oil

Wild Rice and Cranberry Stuffing:

3 cups cooked wild rice

1 cup bread crumbs

1 cup sweetened dried cranberries

½ cup chopped walnuts

½ cup fresh chopped apples (peeled and cored)

½ cup melted butter

¼ cup orange juice

¼ cup cranberry juice cocktail

Directions:

Chicken:

Heat oven to 350°F. With a sharp knife, cut a pocket down the side of the chicken breast about ¾ of the way through. Stuff with Wild Rice and Cranberry Stuffing.

Heat large skillet over medium-high heat for one minute, then add 2 tablespoons of olive oil. Dip stuffed chicken breast in egg wash, and dredge through flour.

Place stuffed chicken breast in hot skillet. Brown stuffed chicken breast for one minute on each side, remove from skillet, and place in shallow baking dish.

Bake in 350°F oven for 30 minutes.

Remove from oven and slice each breast crosswise about ½-inch thick. Place on serving platter over greens.

Makes 6 servings.

Wild Rice and Cranberry Stuffing:

Combine all ingredients in mixing bowl and mix well.

After stuffing chicken breasts, freeze remaining stuffing for future use.

Roast Turkey with Honey Cranberry Relish

(Courtesy of the National Honey Board)

Ingredients:

1 medium orange
12 ounces fresh whole cranberries
¾ cup honey
2 pounds sliced, roasted turkey breast

Directions:

Quarter and slice unpeeled orange, removing seeds. Coarsely chop orange and cranberries. Place in medium saucepan and stir in honey. Bring to a boil over medium-high heat. Cook 3 to 4 minutes; cool. Serve over turkey.

Makes 8 servings.

Roasted Duck with Currant Jelly Sauce

Ingredients:

Roast Duck:

1 duck, washed and dried
6 cups bread crumbs
6 ounces butter
2 onions, chopped
1 teaspoon sage
1 teaspoon pepper
1 teaspoon salt
Water, salt, butter, and flour
for basting

Currant Jelly Sauce:

3 tablespoons butter
1 onion
1 tablespoon flour
1 bay leaf
1 sprig celery
1 pint poultry stock
2 tablespoons vinegar
½ cup currant jelly
Salt and pepper to taste

Directions:

Roast Duck:

Clean the duck thoroughly, and wipe dry. Cut the neck close to
the back, beat the breast-bone flat with a rolling pin, and tie
the wings and legs securely. In a bowl, mix together the bread
crumbs, butter, onions, sage, pepper, and salt. Lightly stuff the
bird with the dressing and sew up the openings to keep the fla-
vor in and the fat out. Place in a baking pan, with a little water,
and baste frequently with salt and water—you may also add
onion and vinegar if you desire. Turn the duck often, so that the
sides and back will be browned. When nearly done, baste with
butter and a little flour. Young ducks should roast 25 to 30 minutes, and full-grown ones for about 1 hour, depending on size.
Serve with the Currant Jelly Sauce.

Currant Jelly Sauce:

Cook the butter and onion until the latter begins to color. Add
the flour and herbs. Stir until brown; add the stock and vinegar,
and simmer 20 minutes. Strain and skim off all the fat. Add
the jelly and stir over heat until it is melted. Serve with roasted
duck or turkey.

Side Dishes & Snacks

Currant Fritters

Ingredients:

2 cups milk

2 cups dry fine bread crumbs

1 tablespoon butter

5 eggs, whites whipped and yolks strained

½ cup powdered sugar

¼ teaspoon cinnamon

¼ teaspoon nutmeg

2 tablespoons flour

½ pound currant, washed and dried

Directions:

Boil the milk and pour over the bread crumbs. Stir well and add butter. Let it cool. Next, beat in the egg yolks, sugar, spices, flour, and stiff whites. Dredge the currants with flour and then mix them in. The batter should be thick. Drop in large spoonfuls onto a greased griddle and fry. Drain them and serve hot.

Cranberry Couscous

(Courtesy of Cape Cod Cranberry Growers' Association, Carver, MA, www.cranberries.org)

Ingredients:

2 tablespoons olive oil
¼ cup chopped white onion
½ cup sweetened dried cranberries
¼ cup chopped pistachios
1 cup couscous
1½ cups cranberry juice cocktail, heated to a simmer
2 scallions, green parts only
Salt and pepper to taste

Directions:

In a medium saucepan add olive oil. Add the white onion, sweetened dried cranberries, and pistachios, then sauté gently over low heat until onion is translucent and slightly fragrant. Add the couscous and the warm cranberry juice cocktail. Stir with a fork to combine, cover. Let sit for 10 minutes. Add the scallions. Fluff with fork. Season to taste with salt and pepper. Toss gently to combine. Turn into serving dish. Serve hot.

Makes 4 servings.

Sweet Potato Soufflé

(Courtesy of Cape Cod Cranberry Growers' Association, Carver, MA, www.cranberries.org)

Ingredients:

6 medium sweet potatoes
½ teaspoon salt
2 tablespoons butter
1 egg, beaten
½ cup raisins
3 tablespoons grated orange zest
¼ cup whipping cream or half and half
Pinch freshly grated nutmeg
2 cups fresh cranberries, chopped
1 cup miniature marshmallows

Directions:

Boil the potatoes with skins on until tender. Peel and mash. Place potatoes and remaining ingredients, except the marshmallows, into large mixing bowl and whip with electric mixer until light and fluffy. Place in baking dish and top with marshmallows. Bake at 375°F for 10 minutes or until marshmallows brown and the dish is hot.

Cranberry-Almond Green Beans

Ingredients:
½ cup fresh cranberries
2 cups fresh green beans
½ cup slivered almonds
Olive oil
Hot water
Salt and pepper to taste

Directions:
Place cranberries in a bowl and add hot water until the berries are barely covered. Allow them to sit for about 10 minutes. Meanwhile, wash and trim the green beans. Stir fry the beans in the olive oil over a medium heat, approximately 3 to 4 minutes. Pour cranberries and the water into the pan and continue to cook until the majority of the water evaporates. Toss in the slivered almonds and cook for another 2 minutes. Season with salt and pepper to taste, and serve hot.

Cranberry Risotto

(Courtesy of Cape Cod Cranberry Growers' Association, Carver, MA, www.cranberries.org)

Ingredients:

2 cups cranberry juice cocktail
2 tablespoons olive oil
¼ cup leeks, chopped
1 cup short grain white rice (such as Arborio)
¼ cup feta Cheese, crumbled
½ cup sweetened dried cranberries
Salt and pepper to taste

Directions:

Pour cranberry juice cocktail into small saucepan and place on medium-high heat. Bring to a boil. Add 2 tablespoons olive oil to 1–quart saucepan and place over high heat. Add leeks, salt, and pepper. Sauté until leeks are translucent and then add the rice. Stir until the rice is coated with oil. Add the boiling cranberry juice cocktail. Stir. Cover. Turn heat down to a simmer. Let simmer for 20 minutes. Remove from heat, add feta cheese and sweetened dried cranberries, then stir well. Turn into serving dish. Serve hot.

Makes 8 servings.

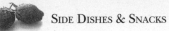

Gooseberry Chutney

Ingredients:

2 pints gooseberries, nearly ripe
¾ pound raisins
3 onions, diced
1 cup brown sugar
3 tablespoons mustard
3 tablespoons ginger
3 tablespoons salt
¼ teaspoon red pepper
Pinch turmeric
2 pints vinegar

Directions:

Mix gooseberries, raisins, and onions. Chop together and heat
slowly with brown sugar and all seasonings. Simmer for 40
minutes with vinegar, then strain through coarse sieve. Seal in
small jars.

Artichoke-Cranberry Stuffing

Ingredients:

8 medium-sized artichokes, prepared and cooked as directed for whole
2 cups chopped carrots
1 cup chopped onions
5 cups bread crumbs
2 cups cranberries, freshly chopped*
1 tablespoon chopped fresh thyme, or
1 teaspoon crushed dried thyme
½ teaspoon ground allspice
⅓ cup orange juice
Pepper to taste

Directions:

Remove outer petals from artichokes; save to enjoy as an appetizer or snack. Remove center petals and fuzzy centers of artichokes; trim out hearts. Chop hearts and place in a large bowl. Set aside. Steam carrots and onions for 8 to 10 minutes, or until carrots are nearly tender. Add steamed vegetables to artichokes; stir in bread crumbs, cranberries, thyme, and allspice. Toss until well combined. Sprinkle orange juice over mixture to moisten stuffing as desired. Toss well; season with pepper. Use to stuff a 12–15 pound turkey, a large roasting chicken, or other poultry. Bake any remaining stuffing in a lightly greased baking dish, covered, during the last 30 to 40 minutes of roasting.

*For easier chopping, freeze cranberries and chop with food processor fitted with metal blade.

Cranberry Rangoons

(Courtesy of Cape Cod Cranberry Growers' Association, Carver, MA, www.cranberries.org)

Ingredients:

¾ cup fresh cranberries
1 each jalapeño pepper
¼ cup sugar
¼ cup mayonnaise
10 ounces cream cheese, softened
1 package wonton wrappers
1 quart frying oil

Directions:

Combine cranberries, jalapeño, sugar, and mayonnaise in a food processor. Process until smooth or to desired texture. Divide mixture in half and reserve one half for a dipping sauce. With the remaining half, blend with the softened cream cheese until smooth.

Lay a few wonton wrappers at a time out on a clean cutting board. Spoon 1 teaspoon of the cream cheese mixture in the center of each wonton. Brush the edges of the wonton with water and fold in half to make a triangle shape. Set aside on a sheet pan lined with waxed paper.

Heat the fry oil to a temperature between 260-280°F. Carefully place the wontons in the oil when heated, and cook until golden brown. Take the wontons out of the oil and place on a paper towel to drain any excess oil. Serve hot with reserved cranberry relish.

Makes 24.

Spicy Mango Currant Salsa

Ingredients:

3 mangos, diced small

½ cup pineapple, diced small

¼ medium-sized red onion, diced small

½ cup currants

¼ cup cilantro, finely chopped

3 tablespoons olive oil

½ teaspoon garam masala or to taste

1 large clove garlic, minced

2 ounces controlled moisture red pepper (about ½ pepper), diced small

1 fire-roasted and seeded habañero chili, diced small

2 limes, juiced

⅓ teaspoon salt, kosher

Directions:

Toss all ingredients together in a bowl, cover, and allow it to marinate for one hour. Taste and adjust seasoning if needed.

Suggested Serving: Serve over grilled light fish such as halibut, cod, or bass.

Cranberry Salsa

Ingredients:

4 ounces 100% cranberry juice blend
1½ cups diced tomatoes
1 cup fresh cranberries, sliced thin
¼ cup ripe medium avocado, diced
½ cup diced pineapple
½ cup thinly sliced scallions (including green tops)
2 tablespoons lemon juice
¼ cup finely chopped jalapeno peppers
2 cloves crushed garlic (about 1 teaspoon)
Fresh ground pepper to taste

Directions:

Place juice into a saucepan. Boil for about 5 minutes until reduced to about 1 tablespoon of syrup. Place the reduced juice and all remaining ingredients into a medium bowl and stir until incorporated. Chill and serve immediately with favorite chips and vegetables.

Note: Fresh cranberries may be stored in your freezer for up to 1 year.

Fruited Rice Pilaf

Ingredients:

2 teaspoons olive oil

1½ cups uncooked basmati or regular long grain rice

1 clove garlic, minced

¼ cup diced onion

1 can chicken broth

¼ teaspoon ground black pepper

½ cup dried cranberries

½ cup raisins

1 cup dried apricots

¼ cup sliced green onions, with tops

¼ cup slivered almonds, coarsely chopped

Directions:

Heat oil in large saucepan over medium heat until hot. Add rice and garlic; cook 1 to 2 minutes or until rice is coated with oil and garlic is fragrant. Stir in broth, onion, and pepper. Cover; bring to a boil. Reduce heat; simmer 10 minutes. Stir in cranberries, raisins, and apricots. Cook 7 to 10 minutes longer or until liquid is absorbed and rice is tender. Fluff rice with fork; stir in green onions and almonds. If desired, garnish with additional sliced green onions.

Strawberry Salsa

(Courtesy of the National Honey Board)

Ingredients:

1 pint fresh strawberries, hulled and sliced

3 medium sweet red peppers, seeded, diced

2 medium green bell peppers, seeded, diced

2 medium tomatoes, fresh, diced

1 large Anaheim pepper, seeded, chopped

¼ cup finely chopped cilantro

½ cup honey

½ cup fresh lemon juice

¼ cup Triple Sec liqueur, or orange extract

2 tablespoons tequila, optional

1 teaspoon crushed dried red chili pepper

1 teaspoon salt

½ teaspoon black pepper

Directions:

Combine all ingredients; mix well. Refrigerate overnight to allow flavors to blend.

Makes 1½ quarts.

Suggestion: Serve 2 ounces of Strawberry Salsa on grilled swordfish, poached halibut, blackened fish, or grilled chicken.

Brussels Sprouts with Pecans and Dried Cranberries

(Courtesy of the American Institute for Cancer Research,
www.aicr.org)

Ingredients:

1 (16 oz.) bag frozen, petit baby Brussels sprouts
1 tablespoon extra virgin olive oil
2 teaspoon balsamic vinegar
2 tablespoons finely chopped, lightly toasted pecans
¼ cup dried cranberries
Salt and freshly ground black pepper to taste

Directions:

Cook Brussels sprouts according to package directions. Meanwhile, in small bowl, stir together oil, vinegar, pecans, and cranberries. Transfer cooked sprouts to serving dish. Gently toss with dressing. Season with salt and pepper and serve immediately.

Whole-Grain Stuffing with Cranberries and Walnuts

(Courtesy of the American Institute for Cancer Research, www.aicr.org)

Ingredients:

1 (24 oz.) loaf sliced 100% whole-wheat bread, one day old

2 cups dried cranberries or mix of dried cranberries, cherries and golden raisins

2 teaspoons canola oil

1 medium onion, chopped

1 bunch scallions (green onions), trimmed and finely chopped

2 teaspoons dried thyme, or to taste

½ cup chopped walnuts

¼ cup finely chopped flat-leaf parsley

¼ cup chopped fresh chives

3½ cups canned non-fat, reduced-sodium chicken broth, heated until hot

Salt and freshly ground black pepper, to taste

Directions:

Preheat oven to 250°F. Arrange bread slices on oven rack and leave in oven until very dry but not brown, about 30 minutes. Shut off oven and allow bread to cool until easily handled. Transfer bread to large bowl. Turn oven back on and preheat to 325°F. Meanwhile, place dried fruit in large, heat-proof bowl and cover with very hot water. Let stand until water is lukewarm. Drain and set fruit aside in large bowl. Heat a non-stick pan over medium-high heat until very hot. Place oil in pan and heat until very hot. Add onion and sauté, stirring constantly, until onion is translucent and golden. Stir in scallions and thyme. With slotted spoon, transfer mixture to bowl containing drained fruit. In a large bowl break bread into coarse crumbs. Mix in dried fruit and sautéed onions. Mix in walnuts, parsley, and chives. Season to taste with salt and pepper. Tossing gently so stuffing does not get compacted, and constantly so liquid is evenly distributed, add enough hot broth until mixture is moist but not wet. (Depending on type of bread used, additional broth may be needed.) Taste and adjust seasoning if necessary, adding salt, pepper and thyme, if desired. If mixture seems dry, add additional hot broth, as desired. To bake stuffing, lightly coat a shallow baking pan with canola oil spray and transfer stuffing to 9-inch x 13-inch pan. Using canola oil spray, lightly coat the dull side of a sheet of foil large enough to seal pan. Cover and seal baking pan with foil (shiny side out) and bake about 1 hour. If less moist stuffing with a slightly crisp top is desired, remove foil halfway through baking time. Serve immediately or store, tightly covered, in refrigerator for up to 2 days. Reheat chilled stuffing before serving.

Chunky Cranberry Dip

(Courtesy of the American Institute for Cancer Research,
www.aicr.org)

Ingredients:

1 (8 oz.) package reduced fat cream cheese
1-2 tablespoons low-fat milk
½ cup chopped dried cranberries
¼ cup chopped blanched almonds
½ teaspoon orange zest, preferably fresh

Directions:

In medium bowl, place cream cheese and allow to soften at room temperature. Mash and work with fork until texture is light enough to combine easily with other ingredients. Gradually add milk until cream cheese becomes soft and spreadable. Mix in remaining ingredients. Cover and refrigerate up to 2 days ahead or let stand at room temperature 1 hour before serving to allow flavors to blend.

Good for spreading on half a whole-wheat bagel.

Makes about 1½ cups.

Dried Cranberries

(Courtesy of Cape Cod Cranberry Growers' Association, Carver, MA, www.cranberries.org)

Ingredients:
1 (12 oz.) bag cranberries
2 quarts boiling water
¼ cup sugar or corn syrup, optional

Directions:
In a bowl, pour boiling water over the cranberries or submerge them in a pot of boiling water with the heat turned off. Let them sit in the water until the skin pops. Do not let the berries boil or the flesh will turn mushy. Drain. If desired, coat the berries with either a light corn syrup or granulated sugar. Transfer the berries to a cooking sheet and place them in a freezer for 2 hours. Freezing the berries helps in breaking down the cell structure, promoting faster drying. Put the berries on a mesh sheet in the dehydrator and dry for 10 to 16 hours, depending on the make of the dehydrator, until chewy and with no pockets of moisture.

Another method of drying is to turn on the oven for 10 minutes at 350°F. Then place the cranberries on a cookie sheet in the oven, turn off the oven, and let them sit overnight.

Store dried cranberries in the freezer. Keep in mind that dried cranberries can be used in place of raisins in recipes!

Makes 12 ounces.

Make-Your-Own Snack Mix
(Courtesy of NHLBI, part of NIH and HHS)

Ingredients:
1 cup toasted oat cereal
¼ cup unsalted dry roasted peanuts (or other unsalted nut)
¼ cup raisins
¼ cup dried cranberries

Directions:
Combine all ingredients, and toss well. Serve immediately, or store for later snacking.

Tip: Put snack mix in individual snack-sized bags for a great grab-and-go snack

Beverages

Red Cooler

Ingredients:

2 cups cranberries
2 cups raspberries
1 cup 100% cran-raspberry juice
1 cup fat-free raspberry yogurt
2 cups ice

Directions:

Place all ingredients into blender and blend until smooth. Serve immediately.

Currant Julep

Ingredients:
1 tablespoon simple syrup (1 cup sugar, 2 cups water)
2 cups currants
2 cups water, cold
Fresh mint leaves
Raspberries to garnish

Directions:
Begin by making the simple syrup by boiling 1 cup sugar and 2 cups water. Mash currants and cover with two cups of cold water. Strain and chill the juice. Put one tablespoon of the simple syrup in a tall glass, add three fresh mint leaves, and fill with the currant juice. Garnish with three or four raspberries and serve.

Raspberry Punch

Ingredients:

1 pint raspberries, washed
½ cup water
1½ cups sugar
½ cup maraschino cherries, chopped fine
Juice from small bottle of cherries
Lemon juice
Crushed ice
Carbonated water

Directions:

Place raspberries, water, and sugar in a saucepan and bring to a slow boil. When fruit is soft, rub it through a fine sieve and add the maraschino cherries and the cherry juice.

To serve, place ½ cup of the prepared raspberry syrup in a tall glass and add 1 tablespoon of lemon juice, ½ cup of crushed ice, and fill the rest of the way with carbonated water.

Strawberry Fruit Drink

Ingredients:
1 pint strawberries (raspberries or mulberries will also work well)
Juice of 2 lemons
1 pint water

Directions:
Mash the fruit in the lemon juice and water. Strain through a sieve. Chill to serve.

Black and Blue Berry Smoothie

Ingredients:

2 cups blackberries

2 cups blueberries

1 cup fat-free plain yogurt

1 cup fat-free milk

1 teaspoon vanilla extract

2 cups ice

Directions:

Place all ingredients into blender and blend until smooth. Serve immediately.

Berry Blast Smoothie

Ingredients:

2 cups blueberries
2 cups raspberries
2 cups strawberries
2 cups blackberries
1 cup 100% cran-raspberry juice
1 cup low-fat blueberry yogurt
2 cups ice

Directions:

Place all ingredients into blender and blend until smooth. Serve immediately.

Raspberry Smoothie

Ingredients:

1 cup unsweetened, frozen raspberries
¾ cup 100% orange juice
½ cup plain low-fat yogurt

Directions:

Blend all ingredients well in blender, and drink!

Variations: Try replacing the raspberries with frozen strawberries, blueberries, mixed berries, mango, or peaches. You can also replace the orange juice with pineapple juice, orange-tangerine juice, or other 100% juice blends.

Strawberry-Melon Smoothie

(Courtesy of the American Institute for Cancer Research,
www.aicr.org)

Ingredients:

1 cup orange juice
1 cup cut-up cantaloupe
1 (8 oz.) container fat-free plain yogurt
10 ounces unsweetened strawberries

Directions:

In blender, puree orange juice with cantaloupe. Add remaining
ingredients and blend until smooth. Serve immediately.

Strawberry Kiwi Smoothie

(Courtesy of the American Institute for Cancer Research,
www.aicr.org)

Ingredients:

1 cup 100% apple juice
1 (8 oz.) container strawberry fat-free yogurt
2 whole kiwi fruit, peeled and chopped
10 ounces unsweetened strawberries
1 teaspoon almond extract

Directions:

In blender, place apple juice, yogurt, and kiwi. Blend until
smooth. Add strawberries and almond extract. Blend again until
smooth and thick. Serve immediately.

Strawberry Yogurt Shake

Ingredients:
½ cup unsweetened pineapple juice
¾ cup plain low-fat yogurt
1½ cups frozen, unsweetened strawberries
1 teaspoon granulated sugar

Directions:
Add ingredients, in order listed, to blender. Puree at medium
speed, until thick and smooth.

Desserts

Cranberry Sherbet

Ingredients:

4 cups cranberries
2¾ cups water
2 cups sugar
1 tablespoon gelatin (1 envelope)
¼ cup cold water
Juice and grated rind 1 lemon
Juice and grated rind 1 orange

Directions:

Combine cranberries, water, and sugar in saucepan. Cook until cranberries are soft. Put through sieve or food mill. Soften gelatin in cold water and dissolve in hot cranberry puree. Stir in fruit juice and rind. Cool. Pour into refrigerator tray and freeze until firm.

Makes 1 quart.

Papaya Boats

Ingredients:

2 ripe papayas
1 cup (11 oz.) Mandarin oranges, drained
1 banana (small and ripe), sliced
1 kiwi, peeled and sliced
½ cup blueberries
½ cup strawberries
¾ cup non-fat vanilla yogurt
2 teaspoons chopped fresh mint

Directions:

Cut papayas in half lengthwise; scoop out seeds. Place oranges, banana, kiwi, and berries in each papaya half. Combine yogurt and mint; mix well and spoon over fruit before serving. Garnish with mint sprigs, if desired.

Bread and Butter Pudding

Ingredients:

6 thin slices buttered bread
1 ounce currants
1 pint milk
1 tablespoon sugar
2 eggs, well beaten
Vanilla or grated nutmeg, to taste

Directions:

Grease a pie dish, and put in the slices of buttered bread in layers with currants between each layer. In a separate container, add the milk, sugar, vanilla or a little grated nutmeg, and eggs. Pour the mixture over the bread and currants. Bake at 375°F for about 30 minutes.

Cranberry-Apple Pie

Ingredients:
1 pastry
2¼ cups sugar
½ cup water
2 cups apple slices
4 cups cranberries
2 tablespoons cornstarch
2 tablespoons water

Directions:
Roll out half of pastry and fit into 9-inch pie pan. Combine sugar, water, apple slices, and cranberries in saucepan. Cook until cranberries pop, about 10 minutes. Make a paste of cornstarch and remaining water, stir into fruit and continue cooking until thick and clear, about 5 minutes. Cool and pour into pie shell. Roll out remaining pastry and cut in strips. Arrange them in a crisscross fashion over top. Bake in 425°F oven for 25 minutes.

Fruit Skewers with Yogurt Dip

(Courtesy of NHLBI, part of NIH and HHS)

Ingredients:

Fruit Skewers:

1 cup strawberries, rinsed, stems removed, and cut in half

1 cup fresh pineapple, diced

½ cup blackberries

1 tangerine or Clementine, peeled and cut into 8 segments

8 (6 inch) wooden skewers

Dip:

1 cup strawberries, rinsed, stems removed, and cut in half

¼ cup fat-free plain yogurt

⅛ teaspoon vanilla extract

1 tablespoon honey

Directions:

Fruit Skewers:

Thread two strawberry halves, two pineapple chunks, two blackberries, and one tangerine segment on each skewer.

Tangy fruit and sweet yogurt make a perfect taste combination.

Dip:

Puree strawberries in a blender or food processor. Add yogurt, vanilla, and honey, then mix well. Serve two skewers with yogurt dip on the side.

Plum-Raspberry Dessert Soup

Ingredients:

8 medium-sized fresh plums (1½ lbs.)
1 cup fresh or frozen raspberries
3 (3 inch) cinnamon sticks
1½ cups red dinner wine
1 tablespoon corn starch
2 tablespoons sugar
Low-fat frozen yogurt for garnish
Mint for garnish, optional

Directions:

Combine plums, berries, cinnamon, and red wine in saucepan.
Bring to a boil, then reduce heat and simmer for 15 minutes.
Whisk cornstarch with ½ cup water. Add to soup and cook, stirring until thickened. Add sugar to taste. Cool. Discard cinnamon
then puree in electric blender. Chill until ready to serve. To
serve, portion soup into shallow bowls. Add small scoop of low-
fat frozen yogurt to the center of each bowl and garnish with
mint, if desired.

Fruit Cookies

Ingredients:

1½ cups sugar
1 cup butter
½ cup milk
1 egg
2 teaspoons baking powder
1 teaspoon nutmeg
3 tablespoons currants
Flour
Milk and sugar to top

Directions:

Add sugar, butter, milk, egg, baking powder, nutmeg, and currants in a bowl. Mix until well-blended and the dough is soft. Roll it out, using just enough flour to stiffen sufficiently. Cut cookies with a large cutter and place on greased cookie pans. Wet the tops with milk and sprinkle sugar over them. Bake at 350°F for 10 to 12 minutes, or until brown.

Watermelon Blueberry Banana Split

Ingredients:
2 large bananas
8 watermelon balls (size of an ice cream scoop)
2 cups fresh blueberries
½ cup low-fat vanilla yogurt
¼ cup low-fat granola

Directions:
Peel bananas and cut in half crosswise, then cut each piece in
half lengthwise. For each serving, lay 2 banana pieces against
the sides of a shallow dish. Place a watermelon scoop at each
end of the dish. Fill the center space with blueberries. Stir yogurt until smooth and spoon over watermelon scoops. Sprinkle
with granola.

Malvern Pudding

Ingredients:
1 pint red currants
1 pint raspberries
¾ pound breadcrumbs
6 ounces sugar
½ pint cream
2 ounces butter

Directions:
Butter a pie-dish well. Wash and mix the currants and raspberries. Spread a layer of breadcrumbs, then a layer of the fruit. Add sugar to taste and bits of butter. Repeat these layers until the dish is full, finishing with breadcrumbs and butter. Bake the pudding for 45 minutes at 350°F. Once it is done, turn it into a glass dish. Whip the cream and spread it over the pudding. Sift sugar over the top, if desired.

Blueberry Cake

Ingredients:

1 cup butter
2 cups powdered sugar
4 eggs
3 cups flour
2 teaspoons baking powder
1 cup milk
1 teaspoon cinnamon, washed and floured
2 cups blueberries

Directions:

Cream the butter and powdered sugar together. Gradually add the yolks of all four eggs. Sift in the flour and baking powder. Add the milk, alternately with the flour, to the creamed mixture. Stir in the cinnamon and add stiff-beaten egg whites. Add the blueberries, which have been washed and rolled in flour. Be careful when stirring in the blueberries that you do not bruise them. Bake at 375°F for approximately 20 to 30 minutes.

Blackberry Pudding

Ingredients:

1 cup flour
1½ cups fine bread crumbs
½ teaspoon salt
1 tablespoon baking powder
1 egg
1½ cups water
2 cups blackberries, washed
¼ teaspoon nutmeg

Directions:

Add all ingredients in a large bowl and mix well. Pour into a pudding dish and bake on 350°F for about 45 minutes. Serve with the Sweet Spiced Blackberry Sauce (see page 94).

Grilled Fruit with Strawberry Dip

(Courtesy of the American Institute for Cancer Research,
www.aicr.org)

Ingredients:

8 ounces part-skim ricotta cheese
8 strawberries, halved
2 tablespoons plain non-fat yogurt
¼ teaspoon dried, ground ginger
4 peaches, halved or quartered
8 chunks pineapple
4 plums, nectarines, or papayas, halved
¼ cup balsamic vinegar
2 teaspoons granulated sugar

Directions:

In a blender, purée cheese, strawberries, yogurt, and ginger together until smooth. Refrigerate the dip for 2 hours before grilling fruit. When ready to grill fruit, thread pieces of prepared
fruit onto 8 skewers. Mix together vinegar and sugar. Grill fruit
until lightly browned, turning frequently and brushing with
vinegar mixture during grilling. Serve grilled fruit with sauce on
side.

Fruit Compote
(Courtesy of the American Institute for Cancer Research, www.aicr.org)

Ingredients:
½ cup sugar
1½ cups water
1-inch piece fresh ginger, peeled and very thinly slivered
1 cup dried fruit mix
2 cups fresh cranberries
1 orange, peeled and sectioned
1 Granny Smith apple, peeled, cored and cut into small, thin wedges

Directions:
In large saucepan, combine sugar, water, and ginger. Bring to a boil over high heat. Add dried fruit mix. Bring back to a boil and immediately reduce heat to low simmer. Cook, uncovered, until fruit is not quite tender, about 5 minutes. Add cranberries and simmer, stirring occasionally, until cranberries pop. Stir in orange and apple. Remove from heat and allow to cool. Serve warm or at room temperature.

This artful fruit compote is colorful and versatile. It can be served "as is" for family meals; as a topping on angel food, sponge, or pound cake for company; or for those favorite winter comfort foods, rice and tapioca pudding.

New England Holiday Pudding

(Courtesy of the American Institute for Cancer Research,
www.aicr.org)

Ingredients:

½ cup yellow (enriched) cornmeal
5 cups reduced-fat milk, scalded (see Note)
½ cup molasses
½ teaspoon salt
½ teaspoon ground ginger
½ teaspoon ground nutmeg
½ teaspoon ground cinnamon
3 cups fresh fruit (peaches, pears, strawberries, raspberries,
blueberries, cranberries, etc.), lightly sweetened to taste

Directions:

Preheat oven to 300°F. Coat a baking pan or casserole with
cooking oil spray.

Put cornmeal in top of a double boiler and hot water in the bottom pot. Set over medium high heat and bring water to a simmer. Meanwhile, heat milk until hot and tiny bubbles form along
the sides. (Do not let it come to a boil.) Stir milk into cornmeal,
blending well. Cook over hot water for 20 minutes, stirring occasionally. Add molasses, salt, ginger, nutmeg, and cinnamon.

Pour into baking pan and bake 2 – 2½ hours. Wash and hull
fresh berries, and lightly sweeten with sugar. Cranberries can
also be used after cooking in water and sugar. Divide pudding
among 6 wide and shallow bowls. Place two or more varieties of
fruit along the edge of the pudding, in concentric circles, placing
lighter-colored fruit on the inside (like peaches and strawberries) and darker-colored fruit (like cranberries and blueberries)
on the outside.

Note: Scalding milk helps blend cornmeal more easily and
speeds the cooking process. Scald milk by heating it to the point
just before it would begin to boil, or when tiny bubbles form
along the sides. At that point, immediately remove from heat
and promptly add to cornmeal.

Tropical Fruit Platter

Ingredients:

1 (20 oz.) can pineapple slices, packed in juice, each cut in half
1 small papaya, peeled and cut into wedges
1 mango, peeled and sliced
1 large basket strawberries, stemmed
Juice of one lime

Directions:

Arrange pineapple, papaya, mango, and strawberries on a serving platter. Sprinkle lime juice over fruit. Serve.

Grape Kebabs

Ingredients:

1 cup chopped pineapple
¼ cup apple juice
¼ cup fat-free plain yogurt
2 small bananas, cut into ½-inch thick slices
1 tablespoon orange juice
2 kiwifruits, peeled and cut into ½-inch thick slices
1 cup purple seedless grapes
⅓ cup small strawberries
⅓ cup melon balls
⅓ cup blackberries

Directions:

For the dip, in a small saucepan, bring the pineapple and apple juice to a boil. Reduce the heat, cover, and simmer for 10 minutes, stirring occasionally. Let stand about 25 minutes or until cool. Transfer the pineapple mixture to a blender or food processor. Add the yogurt and blend or process until smooth. If desired, cover and chill in the refrigerator before serving. Place the bananas in a small bowl. Drizzle with the orange juice, then gently toss until coated. Cut the kiwi slices into quarters. For the kebabs, thread the grapes, bananas, kiwi, strawberries, melon balls, and blackberries onto 4-inch bamboo skewers. Serve with the dip.

Breads

Currant Sweet Biscuits

Ingredients:
¾ cup flour
1 teaspoon salt
½ cup sugar
3 tablespoons baking powder
4 tablespoons shortening
1 egg
1 cup milk
1 cup currants, washed

Directions:
Sift all dry ingredients together, except for currants. Beat in shortening, egg, and milk. Add the currants and work dough in the bowl until smooth. Turn the dough onto a lightly floured board and cut the biscuits. Lightly brush the tops with milk and bake at 425°F for about 15 minutes.

Blueberry Muffins

Ingredients:

2 cups sifted flour

½ teaspoon salt

2 rounded teaspoons baking powder

½ cup butter

½ cup sugar

1 egg

1 cup milk

1 heaped cup blueberries, rinsed and dried

Directions:

Preheat the oven to 375°F. Blend the sifted flour, salt, and baking powder. Cream the butter and sugar, and add the well beaten egg yolk and milk to it. Add the flour mixture and the white of the egg beaten stiff. Rinse, dry, and roll the blueberries lightly in flour. Stir them into the other ingredients. Bake in a muffin pan for 20 minutes.

Cranberry Bread

(Courtesy of Cape Cod Cranberry Growers' Association, Carver, MA, www.cranberries.org)

Ingredients:
½ cup butter
1 cup sugar
1 tablespoon grated orange peel
1 teaspoon vanilla
3 large eggs, beaten
2½ cups flour
1 teaspoon baking soda
¼ teaspoon salt
¾ cup buttermilk
2 cups fresh cranberries, chopped
¾ cup pecans, chopped

Directions:
Preheat oven to 350°F. Spray bottom only of 9-inch x 5-inch loaf pan with cooking spray. Beat butter, sugar, orange peel, and vanilla in a large bowl until light and fluffy. Add eggs, mixing well. Combine flour, baking soda, and salt, then add to creamed mixture alternately with buttermilk, beating at low speed just until blended. Fold cranberries and nuts into batter. Turn into prepared pan, spreading evenly. Bake until wooden pick inserted in center comes out clean, about 50 to 60 minutes. Cool slightly in pan. Remove from pan and cool completely on wire rack.

Makes 1 loaf.

Strawberry Shortcake

<u>Ingredients</u>:
Shortcake:
2 cups flour
4 teaspoons baking powder
½ teaspoon salt
1 tablespoon sugar
¼ cup butter
¾ cup milk

Topping:
1½ – 2 pints strawberries, cleaned and drained
Sugar to taste

<u>Directions:</u>
Shortcake:
Mix flour, baking powder, salt, and sugar. Work in butter and then add milk to the mixture. Toss the dough on a floured board, dividing in two parts. Pat, roll out, and place in two cake tins. Bake at 400°F for 12 minutes.

Topping:
Meanwhile, hull and slice the strawberries. Sweeten them to taste with sugar. While the shortbread is still hot, spread butter on both layers. Crush the berries slightly and put them between and on top of the two layers of shortcake. Serve plain, or with whipped cream.

Cranberry Swirl Bread

(Courtesy of Cape Cod Cranberry Growers' Association, Carver,
MA, www.cranberries.org)

Ingredients:

Starter:
1 ½ cups white whole-wheat flour
¾ cup cool water
Pinch instant yeast

Bread:
All of the starter
2 cups white whole-wheat flour*
¼ cup all-purpose flour**
1 egg
¼ cup evaporated milk
3 tablespoons honey
½ teaspoon instant yeast
1 teaspoon salt
½ teaspoon lemon zest
¼ cup unsalted butter, softened
¾ cup dried sweetened cranberries

Filling:
½ cup white sugar
2 teaspoon ground cinnamon
⅛ teaspoon ground cardamom, optional
1 tablespoon all-purpose flour
1 egg
1 tablespoon water

Directions:

Starter:
In a small bowl, combine the flour, water, and yeast together.
Stir until smooth. Cover and let rest at room temperature over-
night, or at least 6 hours.

Bread:
Combine the starter, whole-wheat flour, all-purpose flour, egg,
evaporated milk, honey, yeast, salt, and lemon zest in a mixing
bowl.

Mix on low to medium speed until the dough is smooth and pulls
back when gently tugged on, about 5 minutes.

Slowly add the softened butter while mixing on low speed until
the dough is elastic and cleans the bowl.

Add the cranberries in last and mix on low just until incorporated.

Allow the dough to ferment for 1½ to 2 hours or until doubled.

Filling:

Mix the sugar, spices, and flour together until well incorporated; set aside until needed.

Combine the egg with the water in a separate bowl and refrigerate until needed.

To assemble the bread:

Gently deflate the dough and roll out on a lightly floured surface to approximately 8 inches x 18 inches.

Lightly egg wash the surface and sprinkle evenly with the sugar spice filling, leaving one of the short ends without filling to seal the bread roll.

Beginning at the short end with filling, roll up towards the opposite end, but do not roll too tightly or too loosely.

Once at the opposite end, seal the roll by pinching the unfilled end to the outer side of the roll; pinch the sides of the bread together to keep the filling from melting out during baking.

Place the bread roll in a greased 9-inch x 5-inch bread pan and cover lightly with plastic wrap.

Allow to proof for approximately 2 hours or until the dough crests over the top of the pan by about 1 inch.

Bake in a pre-heated 375°F oven for about 30 to 35 minutes. The crust will be deep brown but not burned, and the internal temperature will register 195°F on a quick-read thermometer.

Remove the bread from the pan immediately after removing from the oven and allow bread to cool on a cooling rack.

* Regular whole-wheat flour can be substituted for white whole-wheat flour.

** If using all-purpose flour in place of white whole-wheat flour, liquids may need adjusting.

Currant Buns

Ingredients:

2 large potatoes
⅔ cake of yeast or 2 (¼ oz.) packages or 4½ teaspoons dry yeast
1 cup sugar
1 tablespoon butter
1 teaspoon salt
3 cups flour
1–1½ cups currants

Directions:

Boil the potatoes and strain the water into a pitcher. Dissolve two-thirds cake of yeast in a cup. Put potatoes in a pan with sugar, butter, and salt. Mash them until creamy. Pour in the rest of potato water, 2 cups flour, and yeast, then mix together. Then cover and set in a warm place for the night. The next morning, add the currants and remaining cup of flour while you turn the dough quickly. This will keep them from settling in the bottom of the bread. Put in hot pans and bake in a hot oven. Serve hot or cold.

Cranberry Oat Bread

(Courtesy of the National Honey Board)

Ingredients:
¾ cup honey
⅓ cup vegetable oil
2 eggs
½ cup milk
2½ cups all-purpose flour
1 cup quick-cooking rolled oats
1 teaspoon baking soda
1 teaspoon baking powder
½ teaspoon salt
½ teaspoon ground cinnamon
2 cups fresh cranberries
1 cup chopped nuts

Directions:
Combine honey, oil, eggs, and milk in large bowl; mix well.
Combine flour, oats, baking soda, baking powder, salt, and cinnamon in medium bowl; mix well. Stir into honey mixture. Fold
in cranberries and nuts. Spoon into two 8½-inch x 4½-inch x
2½-inch greased and floured loaf pans. Bake in preheated 350°F
oven 40 to 45 minutes or until wooden toothpick inserted near
center comes out clean. Cool in pans on wire racks 15 minutes.
Remove from pans; cool completely on wire racks.

Makes 2 loaves.

Cranberry and Almond Biscotti

(Courtesy of the American Institute for Cancer Research,
www.aicr.org)

Ingredients:

¾ cup dried cranberries

¾ cup whole almonds

1 cup sugar, divided

1¼ cups unbleached all-purpose flour

¾ cup whole-wheat pastry flour

½ teaspoon baking powder

½ teaspoon baking soda

1 teaspoon ground cinnamon

¼ teaspoon salt

¼ cup golden raisins

3 eggs, lightly beaten

1 teaspoon vanilla extract

⅛ teaspoon almond extract

For a sophisticated but healthful treat, try these whole-wheat biscotti with almonds and fruit.

Directions:

Cover cranberries in warm water in a small bowl and soak to plump them, about 20 minutes. Drain, gently squeeze out excess moisture and pat them dry with a paper towel. Set a rack in the center of the oven, and preheat to 350°F. Line a baking sheet with parchment paper (or foil lightly coated with canola oil spray). Set aside. Grind the almonds with 2 tablespoons of the sugar, pulsing in 5-second bursts until most of the almonds are a powder, about 30 seconds. Place the nuts in a large mixing bowl. Add the remaining sugar, both flours, baking powder, baking soda, cinnamon, and salt to the nuts. Toss the cranberries and raisins with a tablespoon of this mixture, then stir them into the dry ingredients, mixing well. Mix in the eggs, vanilla, almond extract and 2 tablespoons water. With a wooden spoon, mix until a sticky, dense dough forms, working in all the flour. Halve the dough. Moistening your hands lightly with cold water, shape the dough into two flattened 13-inch x 2½-inch logs, spaced 4 inches apart on the lined baking sheet. Bake until golden and firm to the touch, about 25 minutes. Cool logs on the baking sheet for 15 minutes. Transfer logs to a cutting board. With a serrated knife, cut each log diagonally into ½-inch thick slices. Arrange them cut-side down in one layer on the baking sheet, with slices touching each other. Bake 10 minutes, turn, and bake 10 more minutes, or until biscotti are a honey color and dry to the touch. Turn the oven off and leave biscotti there for 10 more minutes. Remove them from the oven and let them cool on the baking sheet. Store sealed in an air-tight container for up to 3 weeks.

Sauces & Preserves

Red and White Currant Sauce

Ingredients:
¼ pint white currants
¼ pint red currants
2 ounces sugar, or to taste
½ cup water
½ teaspoon corn flour

Directions:
Cook the ingredients for 10 minutes. Rub the fruit through a sieve. Re-heat it, and thicken the sauce with the corn flour. Serve hot or cold.

10-Minute Cranberry Sauce

Ingredients:
2 cups sugar
2 cups water
4 cups cranberries

Directions:
Boil sugar and water together for five minutes. Add cranberries and boil, without stirring, until all the skins pop open, about five minutes. Remove from heat. Pour into a mold and allow to cool before serving.

Raspberry Froth Sauce

Ingredients:
½ pint raspberries
½ cup water
2 eggs
1 teaspoon white flour
Sugar to taste

Directions:
Boil the raspberries in the water for 10 minutes, then strain through a cloth or fine sieve. Add a little more water if the juice is not ½ pint. Allow it to get cold, and then add the previously beaten eggs, flour, and sugar. Smooth with a small amount of water, if necessary. Cook over medium heat and whisk it well until quite frothy. Do not allow the sauce to boil. Serve immediately.

Strawberry Sauce

Ingredients:
½ cup butter
1 cup sugar
1 egg white
1 cup strawberries, mashed

Directions:
Beat together the butter and sugar until white and light. The success of this sauce depends upon beating it long enough. Whip the egg white until stiff and add the butter and sugar mixture. Mash strawberries to a pulp and stir them in.

Sweet Spiced Blackberry Sauce

Ingredients:

1 cup blackberries, washed
1 cup sugar
1¼ cups water
½ teaspoon nutmeg
1 teaspoon cinnamon
½ teaspoon allspice
3 tablespoons cornstarch

Directions:

Place blackberries, sugar, and 1 cup of water in a saucepan. Blend spices and add to berry mixture. Cook slowly over medium heat until the fruit is soft. Rub through a fine sieve

and thicken with the cornstarch dissolved in ¼ cup water. Bring sauce to a boil and cook for 5 minutes. Cool and serve.

Cranberry Conserve

Ingredients:

1 quart cranberries
1 cup water
2 cups sugar
1 cup seeded raisins

Directions:

Place cranberries and water in a saucepan and cook slowly until the berries are soft. Rub them through a sieve. Return to the saucepan and add the sugar and raisins. Bring to a boil and cook for 10 minutes. Pour into a dish and set aside to cool.

Spiced Currants

Ingredients:

5 pounds currants
4 pounds sugar
1 pint vinegar
2 teaspoons cloves
2 teaspoons mace
2 teaspoons cinnamon

Directions:

Combine all ingredients together in a saucepan and cook over medium heat for about 1 hour.

Currant Jelly

Ingredients:
Currants
Sugar

Directions:

Use currants that are not quite ripe and wash in cold water. Do not stem but remove leaves and wilted fruit. Place a layer in preserving pot and mash well. Then add more currants and cook over low heat to draw out the juice. When currants are white, drain through colander and strain juice through double cheese-cloth. Bring juice to boiling point and boil for 5 minutes. Add sugar and continue boiling until it reaches the jelly stage. Once the jelly stage is reached, pour the mixture into hot, sterilized jelly glasses. Allow to cool, and then seal.

Note: Equal proportions of sugar and juice are usually used for currant jelly.

Strawberry Preserves

Ingredients:
2 pounds strawberries
2 pounds sugar

Directions:
Allow a pound of sugar for each pound of fruit. Cook over a low heat with no water. Do not mash in when stirring. When skimming is required, remove pot from the stove so that scum will rise before you try to remove it. When sugar is dissolved, boil fast for 30 minutes. Remove fruit and place in jars. Boil the syrup 5 minutes longer, then pour over the berries and seal.

Honey Cranberry Barbecue Sauce
(Courtesy of the National Honey Board)

Ingredients:
2 cups fresh cranberries

1½ cups honey

1½ cups ketchup

1 cup red wine vinegar

2 tablespoons lemon juice

2 tablespoons Worcestershire sauce

½ teaspoon coarse ground black pepper

Directions:
Combine all ingredients in a medium-large saucepan. Bring to
a boil and simmer, covered, for 20 minutes. Remove cover and
simmer for 20 minutes more or until thickened (mixture will
thicken slightly as it cools). To can, pour hot sauce into sterilized jars, leaving ½-inch head space. Wipe tops and threads
of jars with a clean, damp cloth. Place lids on jars so that the
rubber sealing compound sits evenly on rim and screw rings on
firmly. Place each jar in a pot of water that comes 1 to 2 inches
above the jar tops. Cover and bring to a boil. Hold water at a
steady boil for about 45 minutes. Remove jars from pot and let
cool on a dishcloth with space in between each jar. Store in a
cool dark place. (In lieu of canning, sauce may be stored, covered, in refrigerator up to 1 month.)

Makes 3½ cups.

Serving Suggestion: Serve over turkey, chicken, or pork, or use
as a dipping sauce for egg rolls or potstickers.

Resources

Cape Cod Cranberry Growers' Association
www.cranberries.org

The Cape Cod Cranberry Growers' Association is an organization devoted to supporting and promoting the cranberry growers of Massachusetts. Visit this website to find recipes, events, helpful data and links, industry news, or cranberry producers in Massachusetts.

Eat Well Guide
www.eatwellguide.org

The Eat Well Guide offers a comprehensive search of local organizations, farms, farmers markets, restaurants, and co-ops that offer local, organic, and sustainable food.

Local.com
www.local.com

Search for local fruit and vegetable stands, farms, organizations, and more on this website.

Local Harvest
www.localharvest.org

Use the search tool provided by the Local Harvest website to find farmers' markets, co-ops, farms, and other sustainable food sources in your local area.

National Heart, Lung and Blood Institute (NHLBI)
www.nhlbi.nih.gov

Visit the website of the National Heart, Lung, and Blood Institute (NHLBI) to find extensive research and information about healthy living and the prevention and treatment of heart, lung, and blood diseases. The site also provides healthy recipes and links to other helpful organizations.

State and Regional Berry Producers Groups and Associations:

California Strawberry Commission
www.calstrawberry.com

Cape Cod Cranberry Growers' Association
www.cranberries.org

Cornell Fruit
www.fruit.cornell.edu

Florida Strawberry Growers' Association
www.flastrawberry.com

Georgia Fruit and Vegetable Growers' Association
http://gfvga.org

Minnesota Fruit and Vegetable Growers' Association
www.mfvga.org

North American Raspberry & Blackberry Association
www.raspberryblackberry.com

North American Strawberry Growers' Association
www.nasga.org

North Carolina Strawberry Association
www.ncstrawberry.com

Oregon Raspberry and Blackberry Commission
www.oregon-berries.com

Oregon Strawberry Commission
www.oregon-strawberries.org

Washington Red Raspberry Commission
www.red-raspberry.org

Wisconsin Berry Growers' Association
www.wiberries.org